Kali Linux for Beginners

Computer Hacking & Programming Guide with Practical Examples of Wireless Networking Hacking & Penetration Testing with Kali Linux to Understand the Basics of Cyber Security

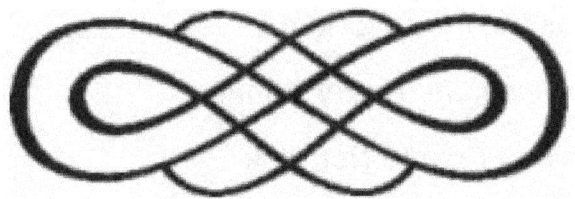

Learn Computer Hacking In Deep

Table of Contents

Introduction 7

Chapter 1: Installing and Downloading Kali Linux 8

Chapter 2: Troubleshooting Installations 12

Chapter 3: Kali Linux External Boot Drive 16

Chapter 4: Basics 20

Chapter 5: Real World Application of Kali Linux and Other Useful Tools 49

Chapter 6: Programming Linux 53

Chapter 7: Basics of Networking 76

Chapter 8: Proxies and Proxy Chains 80

Chapter 9: Virtual Private Network 84

Chapter 10: Introduction to Wireless Networking   87

Conclusion   100

© Copyright 2019 by *Learn Computer Hacking In Deep* - All rights reserved.

This eBook is provided with the sole purpose of providing relevant information on a specific topic for which every reasonable effort has been made to ensure that it is both accurate and reasonable. Nevertheless, by purchasing this eBook you consent to the fact that the author, as well as the publisher, are in no way experts on the topics contained herein, regardless of any claims as such that may be made within. As such, any suggestions or recommendations that are made within are done so purely for entertainment value. It is recommended that you always consult a professional prior to undertaking any of the advice or techniques discussed within.

This is a legally binding declaration that is considered both valid and fair by both the Committee of Publishers Association and the American Bar Association and should be considered as legally binding within the United States.

The reproduction, transmission, and duplication of any of the content found herein, including any specific or extended information will be done as an illegal act regardless of the end from the information ultimately takes. This includes copied versions of the work both physical, digital and audio unless express consent of the Publisher is provided beforehand. Any additional rights reserved.

Furthermore, the information that can be found within the pages described forthwith shall be considered both accurate and truthful when it comes to the recounting of facts. As such, any use, correct or incorrect, of the provided information will render the Publisher free of responsibility as to the actions taken outside of their direct purview. Regardless, there are zero scenarios where the original author or the Publisher can be deemed liable in any fashion for any damages or hardships that may result from any of the information discussed herein. Additionally, the information in the following pages is intended only for informational purposes and should thus be thought of as universal. As befitting its nature, it is presented without assurance regarding its prolonged validity or interim quality. Trademarks that are mentioned are done without written consent and can in no way be considered an endorsement from the trademark holder.

Download the Audio Book Version of This Book for FREE

If you love listening to audio books on-the-go, I have great news for you. You can download the audio book version of this book for FREE just by signing up for a FREE 30-day audible trial! See below for more details!

Audible Trial Benefits

As an audible customer, you will receive the below benefits with your 30-day free trial:

- FREE audible book copy of this book

- After the trial, you will get 1 credit each month to use on any audiobook
- Your credits automatically roll over to the next month if you don't use them
- Choose from Audible's 200,000 + titles
- Listen anywhere with the Audible app across multiple devices
- Make easy, no-hassle exchanges of any audiobook you don't love
- Keep your audiobooks forever, even if you cancel your membership
- And much more

Click the links below to get started!

For Audible US

For Audible UK

For Audible FR

For Audible DE

Introduction

Congratulations on downloading the eBook copy of *"Kali Linux for Beginners: Computer Hacking & Programming Guide with Practical Examples of Wireless Networking Hacking & Penetration Testing with Kali Linux to Understand the Basics of Cybersecurity"*. I am really delighted to see that you have shown great interest in getting to know about the basics of Kali Linux along with all its usefulness in the world of technology today. It can be regarded among the most effective software in today's world. Many even regard Kali Linux as a great boon for the people concerned with computing and networking.

Kali Linux functions as a software for auditing of security and also works from the perspective of networking and hacking. This powerful software comes packed up with lots of security along with information based tasks like security research, reverse engineering and penetration testing. Computer forensics is also a part of this software.

This software is a member of the Linux family. Linux distribution is primarily concerned with cyber security. Most of the big companies today seek the help of Kali Linux for the purpose of tracing and checking the various forms of vulnerabilities which are present within a system. Kali Linux falls under the category of open-source program and it is absolutely free. Kali Linux is a 100% legal software and it is being used for a variety of scenarios within organizations.

Every effort has been made towards making this book as interesting as possible. Hope you can gain a wide amount of knowledge about Kali Linux. Enjoy!

Chapter 1: Installing and Downloading Kali Linux

If you want to opt for information security as your career choice, the most important thing that you will need is to install an operating system which mainly functions as a security system administrator. A proper OS will help you in performing the variety of tasks related to information security and will make the time-consuming jobs very easy. In today's world of information security, you can find a wide range of operating systems among which Kali Linux is regarded as the best of all.

It works as a great tool for the purpose of penetration testing and information security. Today, it is being used by most penetration testers along with ethical hackers who are concerned with the security of a system as well as with various other assessments of the network.

Among all other distributions of Linux, Kali Linux is one of the finest and leading distribution which is being widely used today in the world of security auditing. Kali Linux is the one and only operating system which is related to the security of networks and ethical hacking. It comes with loads of tools which are related to command line hacking which is necessary for various jobs related to the information security.

Kali Linux is most commonly used for computer forensics, security of system application, and penetration testing along with network security. Kali Linux is also the prime OS designed for the purpose of ethical hacking.

How to download Kali Linux?

Kali Linux is an open-source software. That means that the OS can be used and utilized completely along with being totally free. So, Kali Linux can be downloaded easily from the official website of the OS. You can install it by various techniques which you can find in the next section. You will come across various versions of the same and you can install the one which meets your needs.

While downloading the installation file, you will also come across some numbers in hexadecimal number which are being used for the purpose of security jobs. You need to properly check out the integrity of the image which you have downloaded. You will also need to check the SHA-256 fingerprint of the installation file.

How to install Kali Linux on your computer?

The overall process related to the installation of Kali Linux on your computer is super easy. You can choose any of the options which are available for installing the OS. The most commonly used installation options are:

- Installing the OS with the use a of hard drive.
- Installing the OS with the help of Kali Linux bootable USB drive.
- Installing the OS with the help of VMware or VirtualBox.
- Installing the OS with the help of dual booting.

Among all the options which are available for installing Kali Linux on your system, installing the OS with the help of VirtualBox and by using bootable USB drive is the most common. Your system requires a minimum of 20GB of free hard drive space along with a minimum of 4 GB RAM in case you want to install the OS with the use of VMware or VirtualBox.

Installation of Kali Linux with the help of virtualization software

- Just before starting with the process of installation, you need to install a virtualization software like VMware. You can also choose other options such as

- VirtualBox which is a product of Oracle. After you are done with installing the virtualization software launch the software from the applications folder.
- You need to download the installation file for the OS which you can easily get from the official website. After that, launch the virtual machine. For this, open up the home page of the virtualization software which you have installed on your system and then choose Create New Virtual Machine from the options.
- After you are done with creating a new virtual machine, select the iso file or image of the Kali Linux OS which needs to be followed by the selection of guest operating system. You also need to configure each and every detail related to the virtual machine, like Kali Linux. You can now easily start the virtual machine related to Kali Linux after selecting the Kali Linux VM. After you have selected the VM, click on the green button Power button.
- Right after the VM has been powered up, you will see a pop-up menu where you need to select your required installation mode in the menu of GRUB. Select the option of Graphical Installation and then select Continue.
- The succeeding screens will be asking you to determine the information related to locale such as your preferred language in which you want to use Kali Linux, your location, keyboard layout and others.
- After you are done with all these, you will need to set up a strong password for the Kali Linux VM. Followed by this, the installer will be asking you to select the time zone and then will pause at the step of disk partition. You can either choose Entire Disk Space or Create Separate Partition for the VM.
- You will need to save all the changes but do not continue with the process as it will completely erase all the data which is present on the disk. So, always confirm the settings first before proceeding further.

- After this, you will be asked to install the GRUB boot loader. Select Yes and then choose the device for saving up the information of the boot loader which is needed for booting up the Kali Linux VM.
- Click on Finish and the installer will finish the final stage procedures.
- The OS can also be installed by the help of a bootable USB drive as well.

Chapter 2: Troubleshooting Installations

Kali Linux has turned out to be a quite reliable software when it comes to penetration testing and ethical hacking. But, there are times when the system fails and it becomes a tiresome job to install the same. There can be a wide range of possibilities behind the failure of Kali Linux installation. This could include problems like incomplete or corrupted iso download, insufficient disk space of the target machine and many others.

The installer of Kali Linux is really reliable but facing bugs or encountering external problems like bad mirrors, network problems, etc. is very common. So, all that you need to do in such situations is to simply troubleshoot the process of installation so that you can proceed.

Whenever the installer of Kali Linux fails, it comes up with a screen which shows "Installation Step Failed". At such a point, you need to know that the Kali Linux installer functions with various virtual consoles: the primary screen which you can see runs either on fifth console (for the installer of graphics use CTRL+Alt+F5) or on the first console (for the installer of texts use Shift+F4).

In both of these cases, the fourth console which can be seen by CTRL+Shift+F4 will help in displaying all the related logs of what exactly is happening within the installer. You can easily evaluate the reason for the installer problem with a more detailed error message such as "the log screen of installer" which indicates that the target machine is running out of space and the installer is unable to proceed with the step.

The log screen of the installer
The third and the second consoles, which are CTRL+Shift+F3 and CTRL+Shift+F2 respectively, host the shells which can be used for further investigation of the present situation in complete detail. Most of the tools of the command line are provided by BusyBox and so the set of features is
somewhat limited. They are enough for figuring out the majority of the problems which you are most likely to encounter during the installation of Kali Linux.

As you click on Continue, which is available on the main screen Installation Failure, the installer will return you to a screen which you are not likely to see in normal conditions, the Main Menu of the Kali Linux installer. This screen will let you launch the steps of the installation one by one. If you can manage to mend the problem with the help of the installer shell access you can easily start again with the step which failed.

What can you do in the shell of installer
With the installer shell, you can easily inspect and also modify the database of debconf with the commands debconf-get and debconf-set. These commands are used for the purpose of testing the preceeding values. You can check any of the files like the complete log of installation, available in
 /var/log/syslog with more or cat. You can also edit any of the files with nano along with the files which are being installed on the system.

Main Menu of the Kali Linux installer
In case you are still not able to resolve the installation problem, you can file a report of the bug. The report of the bug needs to include the logs of the installer which can be easily retrieved with the Save Debug Logs option available from the main menu.

With this, you can export the logs in various ways, like in mounted file system, floppy or on the web. The most convenient way of saving the debug logs is to let the Kali Linux installer start with a hosting of the web server for the log files. You can launch a web browser from any other computer which is also in the same network and then download all the available log files.

Other methods of troubleshooting

There are various other simple ways to troubleshoot the installation of Kali Linux. Let's have a look at them.

- **Downloading the official form of Kali Linux image:** Make sure that you have downloaded the ISO file for Kali Linux from the official website. The image files are available in various formats such as ISO files, ARM images and VMware images. The ISO files are available in two formats: 32 bits and 64 bits. The VMware images come pre-installed with the VMware virtual machine. The image of VMware is available in the format of 32 bit PAE. In the case of ARM images, it is not at all possible to have one format of image which will be working across all the devices of ARM. In the Kali Linux website, you can find ARM images for various devices such as rk3306 mk/ss808, ODROID-U2/X2, Samsung Chromebook, Raspberry Pi and various others.
- **Verify the checksums of SHA1 for the downloaded images:** While downloading the image for Kali Linux, make sure that you check the SHA1SUMS.gpg and SHA1SUMS file which is available right next to the images of download. Before verifying the image checksums, be sure that SHA1SUMS file is the only one which has been generated by Kali.
- **Installation steps verification:** If you are installing Kali Linux using DVD, try to burn the DVD at the slowest speed. Make sure that you have disabled the firewall or

antivirus on the system so that it does not interrupt the writing process. If you are facing a low disk space error, try to increase the allocated space of the disk. Check the space which you have allocated for the installation of Kali Linux. The best option is to allocate at least 20 GB of space along with the space of swap. You can also troubleshoot the installation by deleting and then repartitioning the free space on the disk. You can also allow the installer itself to partition the free space on the disk automatically and this might resolve your problem.

Chapter 3: Kali Linux External Boot Drive

Kali Linux is a well-renowned name in the world of information security. It has been funded and maintained by Offensive Security which is a provider of services related to penetration testing and information security. Kali Linux has become a go-to distribution for the purpose of hacking. Within a few minutes, you can have a functioning box of pen testing along with various sets of tools that you can find anywhere else. Kali Linux comes pre-installed with a wide array of tools which reduces the stress of installing other tools.

Various options available for running Kali Linux

You can have the option of installing Kali Linux completely on your system. But, in most cases, the systems which you need for the purpose of Penetration testing or ethical hacking might require you to still keep Windows or any other OS as the primary form of operating system. In such cases, what you are left with is to use a virtualization tool and then use the same for running Kali Linux within a virtual machine. However, if there is a lack of memory in the system running on Windows or any other OS, it might result in crashing the VM frequently. Another option is to run Kali Linux on an external USB drive with Kali Linux installed on it. The only problem that comes with this option is the lack of encryption.

What is the best option?
Installing and then running Kali Linux from an encrypted form of external bootable USB drive is regarded as the best option.
But, you also need to secure the same. So, for doing that, you need to follow these steps.
- Start by using a USB drive which is owned by the concerned company.
- Perform full installation of Kali Linux to 1 TB USB drive by using complete encryption of disk on the drive.
- You then need to encrypt the data on the USB drive. As the onboard drive is also in the encrypted state by using a different form of encryption, the onboard drive will not be accessible as well at the time of booting to the OS which is working from the USB drive.
- As the USB drive which you are using is owned by the company, the all-over data which is used is stored in the hardware of the concerned company.
- After the entire project is over, you can hand over the external USB drive to the company and all the related information of testing and data is returned to the client.

Getting started with Kali Linux on USB drive

To start the process, you need to download the ISO file of the Kali Linux installer and then burn the image to the external USB drive you are using. Insert the external USB drive into the machine on which you are going to run Kali Linux. Make sure that you insert the USB drive into the system before booting the system.
- **Setting up the drive:** The next step that you need to follow is to set up the drive, encrypting and then partitioning the same. A dialog box will appear which will

be asking you to choose the partition type which you want for the installation. Opt for Guided-Use Entire Disk for the best performance. This also helps in fully encrypting the USB drive when compared to just encrypting the directory of /home. Always remember that the tools of Kali Linux store all the data in various other places other than the home directory at the time of penetration testing.

The next screen will be asking you to choose the disk on which you want to install it. At this point, make sure that you pick the desired USB drive to install Kali Linux and not on any local drive of the system. If you select any of the local drives, you will be wiping the OS from that particular drive. After you have selected the USB drive click on Continue.

- The next window will be asking you how to partition the USB drive. Select All Files on one partition and click on Continue.
- Next, you will be asked to save all the information of partition and then the process of partitioning the drive will start. When you select continue, all the data on the USB drive will be erased. So, before clicking on Continue, select the Yes option.
- The process of disk encryption will start along with the process of partitioning. The drive is completely erased first and then encrypted. This entire process will take a while. If you are using a USB drive of 64 GB, it will take 30 minutes to get encrypted. If you are using a 1 TB USB drive, it will take approximately 10 hours for encryption.
- After the process is complete, you will be asked to provide a passphrase which will be used for encryption. Make sure that you use a strong one as this will be used at the time of booting up Kali Linux.
- Next, confirm the changes and then select Finish Partitioning.

- Now the system will begin the process of partitioning and after the process has been completed, the installation system will start.
- You will also be asked if you want to use any Network Mirror. Click on Yes as this will be selecting the repo mirrors which are nearby your location and will also help in speeding up the process of update later.

Booting Kali Linux

Insert the USB drive into the machine and then start it up. At the booting process, open up the boot menu and select the USB drive which you want to use. Now you will be required to enter the passphrase and after successful entry, the system will start.

Chapter 4: Basics

Before we start with other aspects of Kali Linux, it is necessary for you to learn about some of the basic tools and commands that come with Linux. Let's have a look at some of the most basic components.

Essential Linux Terminal Commands

In relation to the other operating systems which are available in the market and Linux in particular, when it comes to the term Command, it means a line of command for the applications or the functionalities which are built into the shell of the user. However, this distinction is of very little consequence for the end-users.
. Both of them are used in the same way. You need to input the words into the emulator of your terminal and it will provide results as outputs.

Linux commands for management of file system

- **ls:** This command helps in listing all the contents in the current directory. When you provide the same with a path, it will list the specific contents of that path only. Some of the useful options that you need to know are –l and –a, it displays information as a long list format which comes with much more detailed information and also shows the dot or hidden files.
- **cat:** When provided with one single file, this command helps in printing the contents of that file to the output in standard style. When you provide the command with many files at a time, it concatenates them and then the output is

redirected into a completely new file. The most useful is the option of −n which helps in numbering the lines.
- **cd:** This command helps in jumping from the present directory to some other specified directory. When you use this command without any argument, it will return to the home directory. When you use this command with two dots such as 'cd..' it will return you to the directory which is right above the present one and using the command with a dash such as 'cd −' will return to the directory just before the current one, regardless of the location in relation to the present directory.
- **pwd:** This command helps in printing the current directory. This command is very useful when your prompt does not contain this specific information. It is very useful for BASH programming which is used for obtaining the directory reference of the one in which you are going to execute the code.
- **mkdir:** This command is used for the purpose of creating new directories. The most handy form of switch is −p which helps by creating an entire structure of specific nature if it is not present already.
- **file:** The command file helps in indicating the file type. As the files in a Linux system are not under any form of obligation for having the extensions related to the system to work, it becomes hard for users to get the exact type of a file at times. This command helps in solving this form of problem related to Linux.
- **cp:** This command copies all the directories and files. As this command does not copy the directories recurrently by default, always remember to use −a or −r with this command. The −a command helps in preserving the ownership, mode and time stamp besides copying.
- **mv:** It is used for renaming or moving directories and files. Renaming and moving can be regarded as one single operation where renaming is just moving one single file to the same place with a different name.

- **rm:** The 'rm' command is used to delete directories and files. It is a very essential command that you need to know as you will not be able to remove any clutter without this command. However, while using this command you must be super attentive as this command permanently deletes the files and directories. Unlike other commands, this command does not even store the deleted files and directories somewhere else from where you can fish them out after. Once they are gone, they are gone forever. So, in such cases, using the –r switch is very essential along with the command.
- **ln:** This command is used for creating symbolic or hard links in between the files. The soft or symbolic links are somewhat like the shortcuts of Windows which provides a very easy way of accessing any particular folder or file.
- **chmod:** It helps in changing the permissions of users. By permissions it includes writing, viewing and executing files. Any user can change the user permission for the files which he/she owns.
- **chown:** This command is used for changing the ownership of the files. Only the root user is able to use this command and can change the file ownership. For the purpose of recursively changing the ownership for all the files within a directory, you can use the command with –R.
- **find:** This command is used for searching the entire filesystem for some specific directories or files. This command is very powerful in nature not just because of its capabilities of searching but because this command allows the users to execute any arbitrary form of commands on the non-matching or matching files.
- **locate:** Opposite to 'find,' 'locate' command searches the database for the patterns of the file names. This form of database consists of the snapshots of the entire filesystem.
- **du:** The 'du' command is used for showing the directory or file size. Among the various useful options are –s which provides a summary in place of an entire listing, -h which

converts the reported sizes to a format which is more human-friendly in nature and –d which helps in controlling the directory recursion depth.
- **df:** This command is used for showing the usage of disk. The default output of this command lists each and every filesystem, reports the sizes of the same and also the used space along with the space which is available. You can add on –h with this command for getting the report in a more human-friendly format.
- **dd:** This command helps in converting and copying a specific file in accordance to the main page. You need to provide this command with the source and the destination and it will copy the files respectively.
- **mount/unmount:** This command pair performs the function of mounting and unmounting the filesystems. This whole thing can even range from USB sticks to the ISO images.

Linux commands for processing of text

- **more/less:** These two commands are somewhat similar in function and allow the user to easily view the texts chunked as screenfuls. Suppose there is a very large output from some of the commands, like cat for a file and the emulator took some time to scroll the entire text. When you use any of these commands, you can scroll the texts easily now. The command 'less' is newer when compared to 'more' so 'more' is not used now.
- **head/tail:** This is also a pair of commands but in this, both have their individual uses. The command 'head' helps in outputting one number from the first line of a file and the 'tail' command helps by providing output as a number from the last line of any file. The default output number of these commands is ten which can be controlled by using

the option −n. Another switch which can be used with this command is −f.
- **grep:** This command helps by searching the texts for the patterns. By default function, this command looks at the standard input but the users can easily specify the files which are meant to be searched. The pattern can either be a regular expression or a normal string. It can also print out either matching or non-matching lines along with the contexts of the same. When you run a command which provides lots of information as output, just use this command and see the magic.
- **sort:** This command is used for sorting the text lines according to various criteria. The useful switches which can be used along with this command are −n which helps in sorting the numeric values of any string, -r which helps in reversing the provided output and various others. You can use this command while sorting the output of 'du' command when you want the files sorted in the descending order exactly according to the sizes of the same.
- **wc:** The 'wc' command is used for counting the words, the lines, the bytes and characters.
- **diff:** This command helps in showing the exact difference between two different files using line by line comparison.

Linux commands for management of the process

- **kill/xkill/pkill/killall:** All of these commands are used for the purpose of killing any process and then terminating it. The difference between all these lies in what they accept as inputs. The 'kill' command accepts the ID of process, the 'xkill' command allows the user to click on a window for closing the same and 'killall' along with 'pkill' accepts only the names of the processes.
- **ps/pgrep:** It has already been mentioned in the previous command that 'kill' requires the ID of the process. This can be obtained by using the command 'ps' which helps in

printing the information related to the current processes which are active in nature. The command 'pgrep' works in a particular way: you are required to provide the name of the process and it will return the process ID.
- **top/htop:** These two commands are similar in function and both of these help in displaying the processes. It can also be thought of as the monitors of a console system.
- **time:** This command works as a process. You can think of this as the stopwatch for the execution of a program.

Linux commands for User and BASH environment

- **su/sudo:** Both of these commands are different ways of achieving the same thing- running the commands as some other user. Completely depending on the type of distribution that you have, you have seen one or the other but in actual both are serviceable with these commands. The difference between two commands is that 'su' switches the user to some different user whereas 'sudo' runs the commands only with the privileges of other users.
- **date:** Unlike the command 'time,' this command helps in printing the time along with the date for the standard form of output. The output can also be formatted according to the user specification and it includes everything: month, day and year.
- **alias:** This command helps in creating and changing the aliases to some other commands. This means that you can easily provide new names to new commands or you can rename the already existing commands. It is very useful for the purpose of abbreviating the long command strings which can cause problems while memorizing.
- **uname:** It helps in outputting some of the basic information about the system. By pairing this command with –a you can get the kernel information along with the hostname and architecture of the processor.

- **uptime:** This command will tell you the duration for which the system has been running. It is not very important but it helps in finding out the overall time of the system processing.
- **sleep:** This command helps in shutting down the system after a specific period of time.

Linux commands for management of user

- **useradd, usermod, userdel:** All of these commands will help you to add, modify and delete the accounts of the users. In case you are the only sole user of the system, you will not be requiring these commands that much. But, if the system is being used by various users at a time then these commands are very useful.
- **passwd:** This command will allow you to change the password of your user account. As the root user, you can reset all the normal nature of user passwords however you cannot view the passwords. It is of utter importance to change the passwords from time to time.

Linux commands for documentation/help

- **man / whatis:** The command 'man' helps by bringing up the manual for one specific command. The majority of the command lines come with man page. The command 'whatis' helps by providing one line summary of some specific section of the manual.
- **whereis:** This command tells the users where the binary files of executable nature lives, provided that the binary files are within the path of the user. It can also find out the source code and manual page, if present.

Linux commands for networking

- **ip:** This command helps by providing the ip address of a system.
- **ping:** The 'ping' command functions as an important tool of diagnosis. It helps in testing easily whether you are connected with the internet or router. It also helps by indicating the connection quality.

Linux Command Line

Command line can be regarded as one of the strengths of Linux systems. The CLI or command line interface allows the user to be absolutely free of the distros. It also makes the task of interacting with the system much easier. The derivate of Ubuntu uses the same base of codes but all of them come with a completely different set of tools for performing the same job. The various forms of desktop environments on the similar distro will require various ways toperform the same form of task.

As a user, you will need to forget the processes that you already know and then re-learn the processes for performing the same thing as they hop between the distros. The command line of Linux saves the resources of the system which are also consumed by the GUIs. So, in case you are working on a slower system, it is better for you to use command line rather than GUI.

Many people think of command line as being very difficult; however, it is not. It is as simple as messaging your friends where you text the system what to do.

Getting the shell

Shell is nothing but a program which turns the typed text into the form of orders or commands for the computer system to perform. You can use various forms of commands for performing the same task. There are various shells which you can find for Linux but the most popular shell of all is the BASH, written by the GNU Project. . Another form of modern-day shell is the 'zsh' which you can easily install for your distribution.

If you are working on a desktop environment, you will require a terminal emulator for the purpose of emulating the terminal within the particular interface. Different form of distros come with their own emulators: KDE comes along with Konsole and Gnome also comes along with Gnome terminal.

Some of the basic commands

When you open up the terminal emulator, you will be in the home directory by default of the user who is logged in. You can easily find out the name of the user who is logged in along with the hostname. The '$' indicates that you have logged in as a regular form of user whereas the '#' indicates that you have been logged in as the root. Unless and until you are doing any form of administrative tasks or functioning outside the directories of root, never function as root.

This will change all the permissions for all the directories along with the files on which you have already worked on and will make the root the user of all those directories. You can easily list all the available directories along with the files inside them by using the command '/s.'

If you need to change any of the directories, use the command 'cd.' You can also employ the key 'tab' which helps by auto-completing the complete path. You can use forward slash for the purpose of entering the directories. You will not need to provide the entire path in case you want to get inside the sub-directory of the present directory. For seeing the contents of a directory, you will not need to change the directory. Just use the command 'ls' for viewing the contents of a specific directory.

Some Advanced Command Line

Most of the developers who work with the command line of Linux know the basic form of commands such as 'cd,' 'ls,' 'tail,' 'head,' 'cat,' 'grep,' 'find,' 'sort' and many others. The advanced users will need to know how to function with the beasts such as 'awk' and 'sed' or even perl-oneliners. With advanced knowledge of BASH scripting, you will find that imagination is the only limit. Let's have a look at some of the advanced form of command line.

- **watch:** This command performs as a very beautiful program which periodically executes a program and also outputs the contents of the same on full screen. In case you place the command within inside quotes, you can also run more than one command at a time such as watch –n 1 ' ls –la ; echo ; vmstat ; echo; df '. This whole command will be executing a full listing, displaying the statistics of memory along with the disk space. All of these will be separated with empty lines and will repeat after every second. It is a great way of watching large files get copied and also keeping an eye on the disk space so that it does not come up with any form of issue.
- **curl:** Most of the PHP developers are acquainted with the cURL extension of php which is also available for the command line of Linux. In place of writing any other additional program of php, you can simply use this command line. All the options which you will need are available. Enter 'man curl' and you can find out all the possible tools.
- **logsave:** This tool is very important in nature and it helps by capturing the output from a program and then sends the same as a log file. It also adds a timestamp of beginning and end. You can add up the '–a' parameter for appending the log file.
- **lsof:** This command stands for list open files. It displays all the files which the system has opened up currently. It is very helpful for figuring out which processes use one

certain file or also for displaying all the available files for one single process.
- **strace:** The 'strace' command helps by tracing all the calls of the system which are made by a particular program to the kernel of Linux. This indicates that you can see when a program is opened, closed, read, writes, access the files and many others. It is somewhat like running an entire program without any form of cover. For example, 'strace – ff –e trace=open /usr/sbin/apache 2' will strace the apache2 program and will also output all the open calls.
- **z* tools:** You will often need to diff, grep or cat the files which are compressed. In place of the unpacked files, you can treat the files as being unpacked already simply by using the command 'zgrep' in place of grep, 'zdiff' in place of diff and 'zcat' in place of cat and various others.
- **iconv:** This command helps in converting a file which is encoded in one way for converting the same in some other format.
- **nc:** This command is capable of doing everything and can also be used for checking the requests of service and for making sure that the correct headers have been sent out.

Finding Stuff

Most of the people use graphical file manager for finding out the files in Linux like Nautilus in Gnome, Thunar in Xfce and Dolphin in KDE. However, you can also use the command line for finding out various stuff in Linux which does not even depend on the type of desktop manager that you use.

By using the command 'find'

The command 'find' will allow you to search for the files for which you already know the probable filenames. The command in its simplest form searches for all the files within the present directory and then through the sub-directories of the same depending on your search criteria. You can search out for the files by using the name, group, owner, type, date,
permissions and various other criteria. Enter a dot (.) after the command as 'find.' which will be listing all the files in the present directory which has been found. In order to find a file which matches with some particular pattern, you can use the argument '–name.' You can provide the metacharacters of the filename like * but you will need to put '\' in front of them or enclose the same within quotes. In case the find command cannot locate any of the files which are matching with your criteria, it will produce no output.

Using the command 'locate'
The command 'locate' is much faster when compared to 'find' as it employs a past built database, where the command 'find' searches within the real system along all the actual files and directories.
This command returns a large list of all the names of the paths which also contains the specific character groups. The simplest form of this command finds out all the files within the file system which starts at the root. In case you want to find all the directories or files which contains the proper and only the criteria of search which you have provided, use the argument '–b' along with the command as: locate –b '\yourdata'. The backslash which has been used in the command line acts as a globbing character which gives a way for expanding the characters of wildcard within a file name of non-specific nature into a set of filenames of specific nature.

A wildcard is nothing but a symbol which can be easily replaced by one or more than one characters when the overall expression is being evaluated. The most widely used form of wildcard symbols are '?' which indicates one single character and '*' which indicates a long string of characters. The command 'mlocate' is a new form of the 'locate' command. It helps in indexing the complete file system. However, the results of search include only the files which the current user has access to. Whenever you update the database of 'mlocate,' it will keep the timestamp information within the database.

Using the command 'which'
This command returns the exact path of the executable which is being called when any command is issued.

The 'which' command is very useful for finding out the location of any executable for the purpose of creating a shortcut of the program on the user desktop, on any panel or on some other place within the desktop manager. The 'which' command by default will only display the first executable which is matching. For the purpose of displaying all the executables which are matching, you need to use the option '–a' along with the command.

Modifying Files

One of the many things that Linux along with various operating systems provides is the tools needed to create as well as for edit the text files. There are various text editors that can be found today and every Linux user has their personal favorite. Let's have a look at some of the most famous text file editors in Linux.

Text editors

If you are a Windows user then you must be familiar with the classic text editor known as Notepad. Linux also offers users somewhat similar programs such as gedit, NEdit and geany. All of these programs are absolutely free and each provides more or less the same service. Such programs come with the facility of syntax highlighting which readily helps in editing the source code along with the documents which are written in any markup language like CSS or HTML.

- **NEdit:** This is a form of straightforward text editor which is more or less like the Windows Notepad. It comes with Motif-style of the interface.
- **Geany:** It is a Linux text editor which is not similar to the Notepad++ from Windows. It comes along with a tabbed form of interface for the purpose of working with various open files at one time and also comes with other features such as displaying the line numbers in one margin. It uses up the interface toolkit of GTK+.
- **Gedit:** This is the default form of text editor for the GNOME desktop environment. It is one of the best text editors which can be easily used on any type of Linux based system.

Text editors based on terminal

When you are working from the Linux CLI, you have a wide range of choice in text editors. Let's have a look at some of them.

- **pico:** This text editor started off as the editor which was built in the email program which was also text based known as pine. This text editor was eventually packaged as one stand-alone program for editing and modifying the text files. The modern-day version of this text editor is known as alpine. On the system based on Linux, you can install this text editor by using the command: sudo apt-get install alpine-pico.

- **nano:** This can be regarded as the GNU version of the text editor pico and can be taken as the similar program under a completely different name. You can install nano on any Linux based system by using the command: sudo apt-get install nano.
- **vim:** This stands for 'vi improved' and it functions as a text editor which is also used by the majority of computer professionals. The controls of this text editor might feel a bit confusing the first time. As you become familiar with it, it can make the execution of the most complex editing tasks very fast and easy. If you want to install vim on any system which is based on Linux use the command: sudo apt-get install vim.
- **emacs:** This is a very complex and highly customizable form of text editor which comes with a built-in interpreter meant for the Lisp programming language. It is specifically used by computer professionals who work in the dialects of Lisp like Scheme. If you are required to install emacs on your Linux based system, use the command: sudo apt-get install emacs.

Redirecting the command output into text file

When you are using Linux command line, you might sometimes need to create or even make changes to any text file without running a text editor in actual. Here are some of the commands which you can use for this purpose.

Creating empty file with the command touch

For the purpose of creating an empty file, you can use the touch command. This command helps in updating the mtime and atime attributes of the file assuming that the file contents have been changed whereas nothing actually changes. When you touch any file which does not even exist in actual, the system will be creating that file without putting any form of data inside the file. You can use the command like: touch myfile.txt. This command will be creating a new and empty file named as myfile.txt only if that file does not exist already.

Redirecting text into any file

Sometimes you might need to stick the resulting output of a command into a specific file. For accomplishing this motive easily, you need to use the symbol '>' for redirecting the resulting output to some specific file. For example, the command echo is being used for echoing text as the output. So, the command will be: echo "example text". This command will print the text on your screen and then will return to the command prompt. For redirecting this same output to a file you can use >. For example, echo "example text">myfile.txt. This will be putting the text "example text" into a file named as myfile.txt. In case the file myfile.txt does not exist, it will be created by the system. In case it already exists, all the contents of that file will be overwritten; it will destroy the previous contents of that file and replace it with the new text.

Redirecting to the end of any file

The operator of redirect >> is somewhat similar to the >. However, in place of just overwriting the contents of a file, this command appends the brand new data to the end position of that file. For example, ls –l>>directory.txt. This command will be taking the output from ls-l and then will add it to the file directory.txt. If the file does not exist, it will be created by the system. If it already exists in the system, the output of ls-l will be attached to the file end, after one line of the already existing file contents.

Adding and Removing Software

If you have been using a Linux based system for a long time, you must have known that there are ways of doing the same thing in Linux. This includes installing software applications onto a machine based on Linux by using the command line. The majority of the Linux based users opt for the CLI to install new software in the system. Among the most commonly used methods for installing the software from the CLI is via the software repositories which is where the software files are stored. It is done by using package manager. All the software based on Linux is being distributed as packages which are nothing but files which are associated with the management system of packages. Each and every distribution of Linux comes along with a management system for the packages, however, all of them are not the same.

What is the package management system?

Package management systems consists of a set of tools along with various file formats which are utilized together for installing, updating and uninstalling Linux based software. The two most commonly found systems of package management are from Debian and Red Hat. CentOS, Red Hat and Fedora use the rpm system of files in which the files are in the .rpm format while Ubuntu, Mint and Debian use the dpkg system of files in which the files are in the .deb format. The main difference of all these systems is the way you are going to install and maintain them.

The inside contents of the .deb or .rpm files are somewhat like the old files of archive like the .zip which contains the code of the applications, the methods of installing the software, the dependencies and the location of where the configuration files need to be placed. The software which executes and reads all of the above mentioned instructions is known as the package manager.

Ubuntu, Debian, Mint and various others
Ubuntu, Debian, Mint and the rest of the Debian based distributions use the .deb format of files, along with the dpkg system of package management. There are two different ways of installing the applications through this system.
You can employ the apt application to install the repository or you can also use the dpkg applications to install the apps from the .deb files. Let's see how to perform both the functions.

Installing the applications by using the apt command is very easy:

$ sudo apt upgrade

If you want to update only one application:

$ sudo apt update app_name

In case the application which you want to install in the system is not readily available within the repository of Debian and is available as .deb download:

$ sudo dpkg –i app_name.deb

Red Hat, Fedora and CentOS

Red Hat uses various systems of package management, by default. All these systems use their own terminologies but are still somewhat similar to each other and with the ones which are used in Debian. For instance, you can use either dnf or yum manager for installing the applications.

$ sudo yum install app_name
$ sudo dnf install app_name

The applications which are in the .rpm format can also be upgraded in the system with the help of the rpm command.

$ sudo rpm –i app_name.rpm

If you want to remove some of the unwanted applications from the system then:

$ sudo yum remove app_name
$ sudo dnf remove app_name

When you want to update the applications:

$ yum update
$ sudo dnf upgrade – refresh

Uninstalling software from Linux system

You can install the software in the Linux system by using the repositories of the software. For viewing all the installed packages in the system you can use the command dpkg and then press Ctrl+Alt+T to open the terminal window. So, you can use the command like:

dpkg – list

You can scroll through the complete list of all the packages which have been installed in the system in the terminal window to find out what you want to uninstall from the system.

For uninstalling a package or program, you need to use the command apt-get which is the basic command for the purpose of installing as well as for manipulating all the programs which have been installed already. For instance, this command will be uninstalling gimp and will also delete all its configurations by using the -- purge command:

sudo apt-get -- purge remove gimp

You will need to enter your password here and then hit Enter. The process of uninstalling the program will start and the summary of the required actions which needs to be taken will be displayed on the screen. If you are asked if you want to continue with the process, type 'y' and then hit Enter. The process will continue. After the process is over, type 'exit' in the prompt and then hit Enter. It will close the terminal window. In case you do not want to wipe out the files of configuration, you will just need to leave out the -- purge command:

sudo apt-get remove gimp

When you are uninstalling any program, there might be other packages on which the uninstalled set of program was dependent. F

For removing any of the unused packages in the systems, you can use autoremove command:

sudo apt-get autoremove

You can also combine two commands together for the purpose of removing any program along with its dependencies which are not used any longer by:

sudo apt-get purge – auto-remove gimp

In case you are running out of space in the system, use the command clean for removing all the downloaded files of archive:

sudo apt-get clean

This command will also be removing the cache in /var/cache/apt/archives.

So, installing and uninstalling software on Linux is a very easy and simple job using the command line.

Controlling Files and Directory Permissions

For most users of Linux, getting used to permissions and ownership of the files might be a bit challenging. It is assumed that for this usage level, using the command line is a must. Although there are several other more powerful and flexible options available, opting for the complicated commands is not always necessary. With help from some of the user-friendly interfaces of desktop, you can easily move to little or no usage of command line. It is possible to manage file ownership and permission as well.

The management of folders and files can be easily done from the inside of the file managers only. But, right before we get away with GUI, you will need to have a concrete understanding of what it is doing. So, let's start off with the command line.

Command line: File permissions

The commands associated with modification of file ownership and permissions are:

chmod: For changing the permissions

chown: For changing the ownership

Neither of the two commands is difficult to use. It is really important for you to understand that the sole user who can actually change the permissions or ownership of the files is the root user or the current owner. So, in case you are user B, you will not be able to make any changes to the folders and files which are owned by A without seeking help of the root or sudo. For instance:

A new folder has been created on a partition of data known as /DATA/SHARE. Both users A and B require write as well as read permissions for this folder. There are various ways in which this can be achieved. If A and B are the only two users on the present system, you can easily change all the permissions of the files and folders for giving them access. You can do this with the command:

sudo chmod −R ugo+rw /DATA/SHARE

In this command, the breakdown of each and every command will be:

- sudo: This command is used for the purpose of gaining overall administrator rights for the command on any form of system which employs sudo.
- chmod: This command is used for modifying the permissions.
- -R: This command modifies all the permissions of the parent state of folder along with the child objects which are in it.
- ugo+rw: This command provides group, user and other write and read access.

  In this command, u stands for user, g for group and o for other. The o or other entry is the most dangerous of all as it will be giving permissions to everyone for the files and folders. The permissions which can be provided for a folder or file are:

  1. r: read
  2. w: write
  3. x: execute

The use of the switch –R is very important. In case you have various sub-files and folders within the directory SHARE and you want the permissions to get applied from the parent object to the following child objects, you have to use –R switch to make sure that the same permissions are being applied down to the deepest folder contained within the object of parent.

Command line: Ownership of file

Changing the file and folder ownership is also very easy and simple. Suppose A moved out a folder for B into the directory named SHARE but A still has the ownership. This whole thing can be modified by using a very simple command:

sudo chown –R B /DATA/SHARE

This whole command line can be broken down like:

- sudo: This command holds the administrator rights as you are dealing with a file or folder which is owned by another user.
- chown: This command is used for changing the ownership.
- -R: This command acts as the recursive switch for making sure that all the child objects obtain the same changes of ownership.
- B: This is the new owner of the file/folder.
- /DATA/SHARE: This is the directory which is being modified.

GUI: Permissions for files

Suppose you need to allow everyone to gain permissions of write and read for the folder EXAMPLE. For doing this within the file manager of your Linux distribution, you are required to follow all the following steps:

- Open your Linux distribution.
- Navigate to the file or folder which is the target in this case.
- Right click on that folder or file.
- Click on Properties from the menu.
- Select the Permissions tab.
- Select the Access Files option in the Others tab.
- Click on Create and Delete Files.
- Select Change Permissions for the enclosed files.
- A window will pop up where you need to select Read and Write option under the tab of Files and Create and Delete Files under the Folders.
- Select Change.
- Click on Close.

The trick comes into play when you need to modify the permissions for a folder which does not even belong to you. For doing this:
- Open up the terminal window.
- Enter the command: sudo –i.
- Enter the command: Nautilus.

The command sudo –i will give you a persistent form of access to sudo unless and until you enter the command Exit for removing the access. Once Nautilus is opened, you can easily modify the permissions for the folder or file, even if the file or folder does not belong to you.

GUI: Ownership modification

You can change the ownership for a file through Nautilus by following these steps:
- Locate the file or folder in the window of Nautilus.
- Right click on the file/folder.
- Select the Permissions tab.
- Click on New Owner from the drop-down menu of Owner.
- Select Close.

Managing User Environment Variables

The most common area in which newcomers to Linux find hardest to manage the user environment variables might also be the most obscure of all. Although the environment of Windows comes with environment variables, most of the users manage their own variables. For getting the most out of Linux OS, you will need to understand as well as manage all the environment variables in the very first place for the optimal form of performance, convenience and stealth.

The environment variables are the form of variables which are being used in the specific user environment. In majority of the cases, the environment will be the shell of BASH.

Every user along with the root comes with a specific set of environment variables which are all set at some default values until they are modified. You can easily change all these values for the purpose of making your system perform more efficiently and also customize your working environment.

Viewing the environment variables

You can start by viewing all the environment variables by simply entering 'env.' You will need to understand that all the available environment variables will be in upper case like PATH, SHELL, HOME, among many others. You can also create your own set of user-defined variables which will be discussed later. The command list will print out various variables which are unique to your system. In majority of the cases, this command list is so long that it cannot be viewed in one single page. For viewing all the variables arranged line by line, you can print out the output by using the command More.

After you have used the command More, the whole list of variables will be filled up on one screen and will stop. It will be waiting for you to hit the Enter key to advance to the next line. You can continue to do this until you have found any variable which you are looking out for. When you hit the Enter key a number of times, you will be finding out a variable known as HISTSIZE. When you again hit

Enter, you will be taken through each and every variable of these, one after the other. When you are using the command More for viewing the output, you can enter q for quitting or exiting and then return to the prompt of command.

In place of just scrolling this long list of variables, a tedious job to look for the variable of your interest, you can also use the command 'grep' which acts as the filtering command and will help in easily finding out your required variable.

Viewing the values of the variables

The command 'set' will be displaying all the names of the variables, but if you want to view the values which are stored within the variables, you will need to enter the keyword 'echo' which needs to be followed by $ sign along with the name of the variable such as:

echo $HISTSIZE

The $ sign indicates that you want to function with the variable value which is available inside and not the label of the variable.

Exporting the environment variables

When you modify any environment variable, it is only for that specific set of environment. In this case, the environment is the BASH shell. This indicates that when you close the terminal, any of the modifications which you have made to these variables will be lost and will go back to their default value.

If you want the new variable values to stay for your next session of the terminal and the terminal session after that, you will need to export the variables. You can think of this as exporting the brand new variable value from the present variable to the remaining system to make sure it remains available in each and every environment. You can do this very easily by:

export HISTSIZE

Now, the variable value of HISTSIZE is set to zero when you leave the environment. However, you can easily put the value of HISTSIZE back to what it was, suppose 1000 by entering:

HISTSIZE=1000
Export HISTSIZE

Changing the shell prompt

The shell prompt by default in Kali comes in the following format:

username@hostname:present_directory>

If you are the root user, it will translate the prompt:

root@kali:present_directory

You can also change the command prompt which by default is setting up the value for PS1 variable. This specific variable comes with a specific set of placeholders for all the information meant to be placed within the prompt. It includes:

\u: Name of the present user
\h: Name of the host
\W: Present working directory

You can change the prompt in the terminal for PS1 by:

PSl= "Best Man:#"

Now, each and every time when you will open your terminal, it will show Best Man first.

You need to note that the prompt will be Best Man when you open up the first terminal which is PS1 but the second number of the terminal will still be the same which was set by default prompt.

Changing the PATH variable

The PATH variable is regarded as the most important of all. This variable ultimately controls the location to which your shell looks out for the commands which you type like 'ls,' 'cd,' 'echo' and many others. In case the shell of BASH is unable to find your command in any of the directories in any of your path, it will be returning an error message as "command not found". In case you want to install a completely new tool named "newtool" into the directory of /root/newtool, you can do this by adding it to the PATH variable by entering:

PATH=$PATH:/root/newtool
Echo $PATH

The new tool will be added.

Chapter 5: Real World Application of Kali Linux and Other Useful Tools

If you want to become an ethical hacker it will not be as easy as becoming a software developer of or a programmer. Ethical hackers, also known as penetration testers, need to have a proper understanding about various forms of fields.
Not only will you need in-depth knowledge about the various languages of programming such as in

C++, C and Python, you will also need advanced knowledge about the Linux environment to get started with ethical hacking.

Kali Linux is a distribution of Linux which comes with around 600 pre-installed tools which are meant for penetration testing. As a beginner in the world of penetration testing, this might sound irritating. How could someone learn to use all 600 tools as a beginner? However, the truth behind all these tools is that you don't need to master all the tools. This is mainly because Kali Linux comes with various tools which serve the same purpose and concept. Let's have a look at some of the best tools that Kali Linux offers for the purpose of ethical hacking.

MacChanger

MAC address can be regarded as the legal address of any system. There are various reasons why it is important to change your MAC address. MacChanger helps in changing the MAC address at the time of penetration testing such pentesting any wireless form of network with filtering of MAC enabled. For using the MacChanger , you will need to follow this command:

~$ macchanger [options] networkDevice

The options which are available are:

-h, -- help: Prints help
-V, -- version: Prints the version and then exits
-e, --ending: Do not change the bytes of vendor
-s, --show: Prints the MAC address and then exits
-a, --another: Sets up random vendor MAC which is of the similar kind
-p, --permanent: Resets to the original form of permanent hardware MAC
-A: Sets up random vendor MAC which is of any kind
-r, --random: Sets up absolutely random type of MAC address
-l, --list: Prints the vendors which are known
-m, --mac=XX:XX:XX:XX:XX:XX: Sets the MAC address as XX:XX:XX:XX:XX:XX

Nmap

This works as a network mapping tool. It allows the user to find out the active form of hosts within any network and then gather all form of information
relevant to the task of penetration testing. The main features of this tool are:

- It helps in host discovery. It can easily identify the hosts in a network.
- It comes with the feature of port scanning. It allows you to enumerate all the open form of ports on the remote or local host.
- It helps in gathering information related to the operating system along with hardware about any form of device which is connected.

- It also helps in determining the name and version of any application.
- It extends the default capabilities of Nmap by utilizing the Nmap Scripting Engine or NSE.

Netcat

This is a network exploration tool which is famous in the world of security and well known in the fields of system and network administration. It is primarily used for checking of inbound and outbound network along with exploration of port. It is also helpful when used together with other programming languages such as C or Perl or along with scripting of BASH. The main features of this tool are:

- It performs analysis of TCP and UDP ports.
- It performs sniffing of inbound as well outbound network.
- It helps in reverse and forward analysis of DNS.
- It performs scanning of remote and local ports.
- It comes fully integrated with the standard terminal input.
- It comes with TCP and UDP tunneling mode.

Unicornscan

This is a type of infosec tool used for gathering of information and correlation of data. It comes with asynchronous scanning of UDP and TCP ports along with the feature of finding out network patterns which can help in finding out the remote form of hosts. It can also provide details about all software which are being run by them. The main features of this tool are:

- It performs asynchronous scan of TCP port.
- It performs asynchronous scan of UDP port.

- It performs asynchronous detection of TCP banner.
- It can detect OS system service along with application status.
- It comes with the ability to use custom sets of data.
- It also supports relational output for SQL.

Fierce

It is a tool used for mapping of network and scanning of ports. It can also be used for discovering the non-contiguous space of IP along with the hostnames across various networks. It is somewhat similar to that of Unicornscan and Nmap but unlike these two, Fierce is specifically being used for corporate networks. After the penetration tester defines the target network, this tool runs various tests against the domains which have been selected for retrieving information which can be used for analysis in later stage and for exploitation. The main features of this tool include:

- It comes with the ability to change the DNS server for the purpose of reverse lookups.
- It performs internal as well as external IP range scanning.
- It performs scanning of IP range as well as of complete Class C.
- It helps in logging the capabilities into a file system.
- It discovers the name servers and also finds out the zone transfer attack.
- It comes with capabilities of brute force by using the custom or built-in list of texts.

There are various other tools from Linux which help in penetration testing as well as for ethical hacking . Each of the tools come with its own set of usability and can be used easily by any penetration tester.

Chapter 6: Programming Linux

Programming on Linux is used for creating interfaces, applications, software and programs. Linux code is often used for the desktop, embedded systems as well as for real-time programs. Linux is an open source OS kernel which is compatible with Perl, C++, Java and various other languages of programming.

How does Linux work?

Linux functions as the kernel of an OS which can also be distributed and shared freely. An operating system or OS is that interface which helps in connecting the users with the hardware of the computer and also supports the running of the applications and programs. Kernel is nothing but the OS core as it manages all the communication between the components of hardware and software.

What are the functions of the Linux programmers?
Starting off with Linux programming employs tools such as GBU compiler and debugger. They help in creating applications for the storage of data, construction of GUI and also script writing. More advanced applications related to Linux allow the programmers to develop software related to Linux. They also optimize the programs which are already existing and also write new programs with
various complex form of features such as multiprocessing, multi-threading, inter-process communication and also interaction of hardware device.

Uses of Linux

Linux is widely used today in various servers, computer security systems and architecture of computer system. It is widely used in real-time programs along with the embedded systems of PDAs and cell phones. Linux programming has also resulted in various applications.

How to develop the modules of Kernel?
Before you start off with core programming in Linux, the best way of increasing your knowledge along with expertise of Linux programming is to start working on the kernel module. The modules are developed independently which works with the Linux kernels for functioning as a compact operating system. The kernel modules consist of various things such as drivers of devices for the several peripheries of hardware, file managers and other low-level features of the OS.

The only barrier that comes at the entry of kernel module is much lower in rate than there are for working on the kernel of Linux. There are several modules which are being developed by various individuals and teams. So, there is no specific gatekeeper at the entry of development.

Logical Breakdown of Programming in Linux

When you are using some of the major forms of operating system then you are interacting indirectly to the shell. If you are using Linux Mint, Ubuntu or any other proper distribution of Linux, you will be interacting with the shell every single time you will use the terminal

Let us discuss the breakdown of programming in Linux which consists of Linux shells along with scripting of shell.

So, before we start, you will need to get acquainted with some of these terminologies:

- Kernel
- Shell
- Terminal

What is a kernel?

Kernel is nothing but a program which acts as the core of the operating system. It comes with overall control over all the elements in a system. It helps in managing various resources of the systems based on Linux:

- Management of files
- Management of processes
- Management of I/O
- Management of memory
- Management of the devices and various other components

A complete system of Linux can be broken down like: Kernel + installation scripts + other scripts of management + GNU system libraries and utilities.

What is a shell?
A shell is a special type of user program which helps in providing a proper interface to the services related to an operating system. The shells accept commands which are readable by humans from the users and then converts those into something which can be understood by the kernel. It can be regarded as the interpreter of command language which helps in executing the commands which are read from the devices of input like the keyboard or from the files in the system. A shell starts when a user logs into the system or starts with a terminal.

A shell can be easily classified into two different categories:
- Graphical shell

- Command line shell

The graphical shells provide various means for the purpose of manipulating the programs which are based on the GUI or graphical user interface. This is done by letting the operations like closing, opening, resizing and moving windows, along with switching the focus in between the windows. Ubuntu OS along with Windows OS can be regarded as great examples which provide the GUI to the users for the purpose of interacting with various programs.

Shells can be accessed by users by using the CLI or command line interface. A special type of program in Linux known as the terminal is provided for typing in the commands of the humans like ls, cat and many others and further which are being executed. The final result is then displayed directly on the terminal which can be seen by the user. Suppose you execute the command ls along with the option –l. This will be listing all the available files within the present working directory in a form of long listing.

Working along with the command line shell might turn out to be a bit difficult if you are a beginner only because of the fact that it is tough to memorize a bunch of commands at the same time. It is highly powerful in nature and it also allows the users to store all the commands within a specific file and then execute all of them together. In this way, any form of repetitive task can easily be made automatic. All of these files are generally known as Shell Scripts in the Linux systems.

In a Linux system, there are various types of shells which are available for the users:
- BASH: Also known as Bourne Again Shell, it is widely used in the systems which are based on Linux. It is being used as the default shell of login in the Linux systems. If you want, you can also install this in the Windows operating system.

- **CSH:** Also known as the C shell, it uses the syntax of the C shell and its usage is more or less similar to the programming language of C.
- **KSH:** Also known as the Korn shell, it is the base of the POSIX Shell standard.

Each of the shells functions in the same way but all of them understand various commands and also provides various built-in functions.

Scripting of Shell

In general, the shells are interactive in nature which means that they can accept the commands as inputs from the users and can also execute them.

However, it might happen that you need to or want to execute a whole bunch of commands in a routine manner, so you will need to type all the commands every time within the terminal. As the shells can also take in the commands in the form of inputs from the files, you can also write the commands within a file and then execute them in the shell for avoiding the task of repetition. All of these files are known as Shell Programs or Shell Scripts. The shell scripts are somewhat similar in structure with the batch file which can be found in MS-DOS. Each of the shell scripts is saved with the extension of .sh file such as yourscript.sh.

The shell scripts also come with syntax like all other languages of programming. In case you are already acquainted with any programming languages like C, C++ or Python, it will be easier for you to start with shell scripting. The shell scripts consist of:

- Shell Keywords: It includes else, if, break and many others
- Shell Commands: It includes ls, cd, echo, touch, pwd and many others
- Control Flow: It includes if..then..else, shell and case loops and many others

You can use shell scripts for avoiding the repetitive work and thus opting for automation. It also helps in monitoring of the system, and allows the addition of various new functionalities to the shells.

Programming in Linux Using C

Linux is turning out to be a heaven of programming for developers. It is mainly because of the open source nature of Linux and also being a completely free operating system. Turbo C compiler is the old form of compiler which has been used for compiling programs. The same job can be done on Linux for creating a new environment of programming. Let's have a look at how to get started with programming in Linux by using C for writing, compiling and running programs based on C.

If you have not yet installed any Linux distribution on your system such as Ubuntu, you can do it by installing any virtual machine on the system like the VirtualBox. It is a product which has been designed by Oracle to allow the users to run any form of virtual machine on the computer system. This means that you can easily run Linux on your Apple or Windows system. After you have downloaded your virtual machine, install it on your computer and then restart your system and then create a brand new virtual machine. For creating a virtual machine:

- Press the New button for creating new VM.
- Provide a proper name to your virtual machine.
- Select the operating system as Linux and Ubuntu 64 bit.
- Click on Next.
- Click on Create Virtual Hard Disk.
- Click on Create.

How to install C language on Linux?

- Open up the terminal window. For this go to Applications then Accessories and then click on Terminal. This will open up a new terminal window.
- For the purpose of running C program in the system, you will need to install the essential packages. For achieving this, you will need to enter the command in the terminal window as:
sudo apt-get install build-essential
It will now ask for the administrator password. After you have entered the password correctly, the process of installation will begin. For the purpose of installing the packages, you will need to be connected with the Internet. It will take some time to complete which will depend on the speed of the internet.
- Now you can write and run your desired program.

How to write programs based on C in Linux?

For writing C program in Linux follow these steps:
- Open up any text editor such as gedit. You can do this by entering the command gedit prog.c.
- Write the program. For instance: #include<stdio.h>int main(){ printf("Hello"); return 0;}
- Then save the program with .c extension.
- Then you will need to compile the program.
- Then you can run or execute the program.

Programming in depth

- Enter the command mentioned below in the terminal window to open up a text editor.
gedit prog.c
- After the text editor has opened up, you can now write the program.

- After you are done with writing your program, save it and then close the text editor.
- You can compile the program as below:
  gcc prog.c −o prog
- If there is no error within your written program, nothing will be shown on the screen. If there is any form of error in your program it will be shown. You will also need to open up the text editor again and then repeat all the steps for removing the error and then save it.
- For running the program enter this command:
  ./prog
- After the program has run, you can see the program output in another terminal window.

Programming in Linux using C++

C can be regarded as a language of programming which is of procedural nature. It was developed between 1969 and 1973 by Dennis Ritchie. Initially, it was developed as a programming language for the purpose of writing up a complete operating system. The main features of the C++ language come with low-level accessing of system memory, a very simple and easy set of keywords and a very clean style. All these features make the C++ language very much suitable for all sort of system programming such as operating system or even development of a compiler. The first step includes installation of some development tools along with several applications like GCC, GNU, C++ compiler for the task of compiling the program and for executing the overall code in Linux. C and C++ are somewhat similar and for understanding C++ let us first have a look at C.

If you want you can also verify the installed set of tools by using the command:

cc –v.

Let us now consider a very easy C program file which is named as Sort.c:

```c
int main( void )
{
 printf( "Hello! Sort\n" );
 return 0;
}
```

For compiling this easy program you can use:
cc filename.c -o executable_file_name
In this command, the filename.c is the C program file and -o option has been used for showing up the errors in the code. If there is no error in the code, it will generate an executable form of file named as executable_file_name.
cc Sort.c -o sortoutput
In this, sortoutput is the file which is executable in nature and it is being generated. So, you can execute the same like:
./sortoutput

For program files related to C++

C++ is a programming language which has been developed for the general purpose of programming and is being widely used today for competitive programming.
It comes with object-oriented, imperative and generic program features. You can run C++ on various OS platforms such as Linux, Windows, Mac, Unix and many others. Before we start programming by using C++, you will need a proper environment which needs to be set up on your computer system for the purpose of compiling and running your C++ based programs. You can verify all your installed tools on C++ by using this command:
g++ -- version
Let us consider a very simple C++ program:
// main function

```cpp
// where the execution
// of program starts
int main()
{
// print Hello Universe!
cout<< "Hello Universe!\n";
return 0;
}
```

For compiling this entire code you can use:

`g++ filename.cpp -o executable_file_name`

Here in this command, filename.cpp is the file of C++ program and -o option has been used for showing out the errors within the code. In case no error has been found, it will generate an executable form of file named as executable_file_name.

`g++ sort.cpp -o sortoutput`

Here in this command, sortoutput is the executable form of file which is being generated. So, you can execute the same such as:

`./sortoutput`

Installing compiler for C++ in Linux

If you are using a Linux based system such as CentOS, Red Hat, Fedora or something else, you can type in this command as the root for installing the compiler of C++:

`yum install –y gcc-c++*`

In order to verify that the compiler of GCC has been installed properly in the system use:

`rpm –qa | grep –i c++`

You can also use the which command as:

`which c++`

Writing the first C++ based program on Linux

- From the terminal window, open up a new file for the purpose of editing by using the command vim as:
  `vim hello.cc`

- Within the vim editor, you can now type your C++ program or code.
- After you are done, save and then exit the file.
- For compiling the new program of C++, you will need to type this command in the terminal:
  c++ hello.cc
  If the compilation process runs without any error, no form of output is going to be printed on the screen.
- An executable form of file will be created within the present directory with a.out as the default name.
- For running this same program, you can execute the executable file which has been generated in a similar way you execute any of the executables of Linux.

How to specify name meant for the executable which has been generated?

Compiling the programs of C++ without any of the specifying options will be producing an executable form of file with the name a.out. If you want to specify a particular name for the executable of your choice you have two ways: first, is to rename the a.out default after it has been created and second, is to specify the filename of the executable at the time of compilation by using the option −o.
c++ hello.cc −o /opt/hello.run

Executing the system commands from programs of C++

It is very important to be able to communicate with the compiling system by executing the commands of OS when needed. The system() function will allow you to run the commands of the system from the code of C++. For the ease of the compiler to recognize all these functions properly and for compiling in the proper way, stdlib.h library file is required to be invoked.

Bottom line
- For writing down C or C++ based programs on the machines based on Linux, you will need the GCC compiler.
- All the C++ programs are saved and written as .cc format of files.
- All the resulting form of executables can also be executed in a similar way the Linux or Unix executables are being executed.
- The system function is used for running commands of the system from the code of C++.
- The g++ and c++ command both compile and link with the source files of C++.

Programming in Linux Using Python

Python is one of the modern-day programming languages which has been gaining lots of traction in the development community. It was developed by Guido von Rossum in 1990. It is somewhat like Java in which the programs, once written can be easily run on any type of operating system. If you are starting off with programming for the first time in Linux, Python is a great choice for you to begin with. It comes with a low learning curve along with an elegant system of coding.

Installation of Python
Linux based distributions such as Ubuntu come with a version of command line pre-installed which makes the ultimate game of starting with Python very easy and simple. In fact, many in the Linux community developed many of the scripts and sets of tools under Python.
You can start the process with either the graphical interactive development environment or IDLE or command line version.

Programming Python from the command line

Open up your terminal window and then type in python within quotes as 'python'. This will open up Python in the interactive mode. This mode is really good for learning at the initial stages, however, you might want to use a text editor such as Vim, Gedit or Emacs for writing down your codes. As long as you save the codes with the extension of .py, you can execute them in the terminal window. Most of
the programming starts with the very old standby: the program of Hello Universe or World. So, we will also start it from there.

At the command prompt, type in print "Hello Universe" and then hit enter. You can readily see the command being printed on the line next to the command. For running a script from the command line just type: python my_script.py. If you want to exit from the command line type in exit () or just hit Ctrl+d.

Programming Python with IDLE
If you are thinking of writing down a long program right from the command line, you can start with IDLE. Just open up the terminal window and then type in: 'idle'. You will now see that the graphical shell of Python has been loaded. For writing down a script in Python, just click on File then New Window.
This will be opening up a kind of text editor just like Notepad. Then, all you need to do is to just type this code:

#linuxversion.py
#Have user input version and response
name= raw_input("Which release of Linux do you see")
print "Even I like", name, " – Linux is great!"

A variety of things are going on here in this command. The first two lines which are preceded by the sign # are just mere comments. The third line will be using the input which has been gathered from the function raw_input and then it will assign the same to a variable which is a name.

At the end, the print statement will return the results. You can save the file with an extension of .py and then select Run followed by Run Module from the available menu for running your program.

Note that there are various programming languages which generally ignore any of the whitespaces which is actually the spacing in between the codes. However, in the case of Python, when there is any form of improper spacing it can lead to syntax errors. So, make sure that you enter the spaces properly for running the code properly.

Python Programming

It is often said that systems administrators are required to be very proficient with the language of scripting.
While most of the people are very much comfortable in using BASH for running the scripts, Python in place of it can actually add several benefits. Python allows the users to access all the tools of the command line and also makes use of the Object Oriented Programming structure. The versions of Python: 2.x and 3.x can be usually found for most of the distributions of Linux. For entering a shell of Python just type in python3 or python in the emulator of your terminal. For exiting from the shell just type in quit().

It is to be noted that while version 2.x of Python is still used today, it is not at all maintained actively. For this reason, it is always better to switch to 3.x. There are certain differences in syntax in both the versions of Python.

You can perform various arithmetic operations along with manipulation of text strings in Python. If you want you can even assign the operational results to the variables and then display the same on the screen. A very handy feature that comes with Python is concatenation: you will need to supply the variable or string values in a list which is comma-delimited for printing the function and it will return the sentence completely composed by the listed items in a sequence. You can also mix up variables of various types and after you have assigned one specific value to any of the variables, you can change the type of data in a later stage without any form of problem.

You can easily create lists in Python. A list is nothing but an ordered set of items which is not at all necessary to be of the similar data type. For creating an empty set of list names as bandsRock, you will need to use square brackets along with the command as:

bandsRock=[]

For appending any of the items to the bottom of the list use append(). For removing any of the items from the list, you can easily pass the particular element to the method remove() or the proper position of the item in the list as pop(). For displaying the complete list of the available methods for any object you can use Ctrl+space after you have typed in the item name along with a dot.

Programming in Linux Using Java

Java is one of the most popular languages of programming. It is widely used for the purpose of developing software for almost everything starting from cell phones to the cable TV boxes and extending its use to the large systems of enterprise information. The overall concept behind writing the source code of Java, compiling and then running it is more or less the same across most of the OS.

Java is one of the most popular languages of programming. It is widely used for the purpose of developing software for almost everything starting from cell phones to the cable TV boxes and extending its use to the large systems of enterprise information. The overall concept behind writing the source code of Java, compiling and then running it is more or less the same across most of the OS.

Java is a programming language which was originally developed by Sun Microsystems. It falls under the category of compiled form of programming language in which the programmer writes up the source code and then submits the same to the compiler which will be checking out the syntaxes of the program and will generate a complete file which you can run. For instance, when you are using Google Chrome web browser, you are in true sense running all the programs which have been generated from a compiler which is used by the software developers.

To a wide extent, the programming languages of the past needed you to re-compile all the source code for every new OS in which you wanted to run your program on. For instance, a program which has been compiled for running in Windows will not be running on a system which has Linux in it unless it has been re-compiled. Given the wide differences in the OS and the elements of hardware, this process was very difficult and complicated to carry out. One of the major motivations for Java was the motivation of being able to write only one single set of source code and then provide the resulting program with the ability to run on some different set of operating systems or environments of operation.

Java comes with write once and then run anywhere capability only because of the way in which the compiler translates the entire source code in a particular file known as Byte Code file which can then run under any form of supported JRE or Java Runtime Environment.

The development process of Java involves these steps:

- Write down the Java source code and then save it in one or more plain text files. All of these files generally come with .java format at the end.
- Run the compiler of Java (javac) for compiling the source code which you have written into a file of Byte Code. The Byte Codes generally have .class at the end of the name of the file.
- Run the program after submitting the byte code to a JRE.

Downloading Java Development Kit

For doing any of the programming stuff with Java, you will need to download, and then install, Java Development Kit or JDE. In most cases, when you come across the installation of Java in a system it means the installation of Java Runtime Environment or JRE. In this example, you will need JDK which comes with a special type of program named as javac which is used for compiling the Java source codes into the class files. You can download JDK from the official website of Oracle.

While downloading the JDK, make sure that you download the one which matches with the operating system that you are currently using. In this case, if you are using Linux, download the file which is supported by Linux OS. Most of the distributions of Linux like Ubuntu, Debian, Red Hat and others, come with a tool of software repository which helps in automating the installation along with the download steps. For instance, under the distribution of Ubuntu and Debian, the command apt-get is used for downloading and then installing JDK such as:

sudo apt-get install openjdk-7-jdk

For installing the OpenJDK under Fedora, CentOS and other distributions which use up YUM, you can use this command:

yum install java-1.7.0-openjdk

Both the apt-get as well as yum installers will be downloading, installing and then configuring the JDK without any form of additional task on the part of the user.

Writing and compiling Java program

The programming language of Java is a form of compiled language in which the programmer writes up the source code and it is then submitted to the compiler. A compiler is nothing but a program which helps in converting source code into Byte Code.
The Byte Code which comes out as a result is executed with the use of the JRE. You can write the source code of Java by the use of any text editor, like Notepad in Windows and in Linux pico or nano editors which are used for editing the files of source code. For starting off with Java program follow these steps:

- Open up shell prompt in Linux. You can also achieve this by pressing ALT+Ctrl+T in Linux.

- Create a new file by using the program gedit by simply typing:
  gedit HelloUniverse.java
  The gedit program will open up and will create a file.
- Type in your Java source code.
- After you are done with your source code, make sure that you save it.
- Exit from the gedit program.
- Now it's the time to compile the program with the use of javac compiler. The command will be: javac HelloUniverse.java
- If there is no error in the syntax, the compiler will run smoothly.
- Now you can run the sample program which you have created by running Java and then followed by the program name.

Java programming also includes another component known as the class. It is a large collection of functions which carries out various work along with templates for the various data which might be carried on. In the program example which was mentioned just before this, HelloUniverse is the class of the program.

Scripting on Linux Using BASH

BASH is an interpreter of command language. It is available widely on various types of operating systems and it also acts as the default interpreter of command for most of the Linux or GNU systems. BASH works with shells. A shell is nothing but a macro processor which lets non-interactive or

interactive form of command execution. In BASH, scripting allows execution of automatic commands which would have been otherwise executed one by one in an interactive form.

Basics of Bash Shell

A shell allows the user to interact with the computer by using the commands. It also helps in storing and retrieving data, processing of information and several other tasks. For example, you can type in commands such as cal, date, pwd or ls and then hit the Enter key. What you have just done is interacted with the system by the use of the shell to retrieve the present date and time.

It was done by using date, checking out the calendar by using cal, checking out the location of your present directory on which you are working by using pwd and then retrieving a complete list of directories and files which is located within ls.

What is meant by scripting?

For understanding scripting in the proper way, first use the shell in combination with the text editor that you use such as .vi for creating a brand new file named as task.sh which will contain all the commands from above, each of the commands on different lines. After you are done with this, you will need to make the new file completely executable by using the command chmod along with an option +x. Lastly, all that you need is to execute the new script by prefixing the name along with ./.

By the use of proper scripting, any form of shell interaction can be scripted as well as automated. It is also possible now to execute the new shell script task.sh automatically daily at any time you want by using cron time-based scheduler and then store the output of the script to a specific file every time it is executed.

Basics of BASH

Till now we have discussed shell and scripting. But, what about BASH? As we have already discussed earlier, BASH is a default form of interpreter for many Linux or GNU based systems. That is the reason why our last shell script worked even without the definition of bash as the final interpreter.

For finding out what is the interpreter by default you can execute this command:

$ echo $SHELL
/bin/bash

You can also find out several other interpreters of shell, like C shell, Korn shell and various others. To define the script interpreter as BASH, you will need to locate first a complete path for its executable binary by using the command 'which'. This command needs to be prefixed with shebang or # !. You will need to insert this at the very first line of the script. There are other methods for defining your shell interpreter, but this is regarded as the best option.

File permissions and names

In order to execute the shell script, your file needs to be in executable form by using the command chmod +x FILENAME. Any form of newly created files will not be in the executable form by default, regardless of the suffix of the file extension. On the systems based on Linux or GNU the command 'file' is used for identifying the file type.

Execution of script
In simple terms, a bash script is nothing but a simple text file which contains instructions which need to be executed in proper order from the top to the bottom. The way in which the instructions are interpreted depends on the defined shebang or the process in which the script is being executed.

There is another method of executing the bash scripts in which the bash interpreter is called in explicit order such as by $ bash date.sh. By calling out the binary executable in explicit form, the file content of date.sh is being loaded up and then interpreted as the bash shell script.

Simple Backup Shell Script

Any of the commands which can be executed successfully via the bash shell terminal can be in the similar form which is being used as a part of the shell script of bash. There is no proper differentiation between the direct execution of

Any of the commands which can be executed successfully via the bash shell terminal can be in the similar form which is being used as a part of the shell script of bash. There is no proper differentiation between the direct execution of
command through the terminal or within a script of shell away from the fact that script shell offers a non-interactive form of execution for the various commands within a single process. Most of the commands accept arguments and options. The command options are being used for modifying the behavior of the commands for the purpose of producing alternative form of output results which are prefixed by -. The arguments can specify the execution of commands for the target like directory, file, text and others.

You can use the command 'man' for displaying the manual page of any of the desired command. For instance, in order to display the manual page for the command ls you can execute the command man ls. For quitting the manual page you can press the key 'q'.

Variables

Variables can be regarded as the prime essence of programming. This allows the programmers to store up the data, reuse and then alter the same throughout the complete script. You can create a brand new script such as welcome.sh by using variables.

Input and Output

The commands which are executed on the Linux/GNU command line either require input, produce the output or display an error message. This is a very basic concept of shell scripting along with working with the command line of Linux or GNU in general.

The commands which are executed on the Linux/GNU command line either require input, produce the output or display an error message. This is a very basic concept of shell scripting along with working with the command line of Linux or GNU in general. Each time you execute a command, there are three possible outcomes: The first possibility is it will be producing an output, the second possibility will be generating an error and the third possibility might not produce any form of output.

Chapter 7: Basics of Networking

In today's world where everything comes with the touch of technology, networking has turned out to be a mandatory component for setting up a new business or organization. Networking helps in seamlessly connecting with a set of related devices or systems with the endpoints or rather the host or master system via various forms. It holds a very important position for all providers of services, businesses and the consumers all around the globe to communicate and interconnect with each other at the same time.

The concept of networking comes along with almost everything such as text messages, calling on the telephone, streaming of video and many more.

The operation of networks comes along with some serious set of skills which largely depends on its complexity. For example, in a large enterprise where there are several nodes along with requirements of network security such as functioning of the administrator, encryption and various others. On the other hand, any person who just uses networking along with the internet for day to day work at home can set up easily along with troubleshooting of the several problems of basic nature within the nature of wireless networks.

Networking basics

For properly understanding the functioning of networking along with its components, you will need to know about the basics. A network of computer systems is built up of several elements which help in the overall functioning.

Types of networking

Networking of computers can be classified into two main categories: wired and wireless. While talking about a wired network, it requires a physical form of network which is needed for the transportation of information between the two nodes. For digital communication in business places and homes, Ethernet cables are being used owing to their overall cost-effectiveness along with durability. Today, optical fibers are also being used for transportation of data across long distances.

Optical fibers also offer a faster rate of speed than Ethernet cables. However, Ethernet cables are much cheaper when compared with optical fibers.

In a wireless form of networking, radio waves are utilized for data transportation through the air. In this, the devices are connected to one another without any type of cables in between them. Wireless LAN is being used most widely for the purpose of wireless networking. There are various alternatives which can be found today like Bluetooth, satellite, cellular, microwave and various others.

After various practical experiences, it has been found that the wired form of networking comes with much better speed and security plus reliability as compared with the wireless mode of networking. But, with wireless networking comes greater probability of scalability, mobility and flexibility than the wired form of networking.

Both types of networking are being classified in accordance with the physical layer of the networks. It can also be differentiated according to the build and design structure of the networks, network overlay and approaches which are made for encompassing SDN. The networks can also be categorized by the scale, WAN, LAN, network storage area, environment and various other aspects.

Networking system and its types

When you come across networking systems you will find two different types: open and closed. Within an open system, the whole system stays connected with the network which is ready for any type of communication. In a closed system, the system stays unlinked with the network and you will not be able to connect with the network.

Components of networking

The system of networking requires the infrastructure of a proper physical form of network. It consists of several networking components like switches, routers, access points and also some basic form of firmware which ultimately helps in the operation of the other connected components.

The other components include the software which is needed for the purpose of security, monitoring and management of the network. Any type of network depends largely on the protocols plus its standards for the performance of discrete form of jobs or for the purpose of communication with various data types. By protocol, it means a proper set of algorithms or set of rules which defines the ways in which the different entities related to communication connect with one another across a network. You can fund several types of protocols within a network like ARP, IP, TCP, FTP, DHCP and various others.

Voice over IP or VoIP is being used for the purpose of transporting the IP telephonic traffic directly to the final point which is also supported by the protocol. TCP/IP is regarded as the internet protocol suite which is responsible for the transportation of data across a network based on IP. An IP address can be regarded as the logical form of address which behaves as the address of the network for all the systems in a network. It provides help in setting up a unique form of identification for each and every device within a network. The IP addresses which are found for the network are in 32 bits structure. IPV4 is being assigned by the IANA for all the systems within a network.

The physical form of address of each and every network host is known as the MAC address. It stays linked with the network interface card or NIC. You can find MAC addresses in 48 bits or 12 nibble. The MAC addresses are assigned to the devices at the time of manufacturing.

Chapter 8: Proxies and Proxy Chains

With advances in technology, the number of hackers is also increasing day by day. While talking about hackers, some are good and some can be regarded as evil. Most of the evil hackers use the methods of hacking for stealing valuable and confidential information, for money or some even hack just for fun. The evil hackers have the tendency to create a situation of havoc in the world of cyber security by spreading harmful malware and other malicious items. The good hackers might also hack for money. But they do it the proper way like taking part in a bug bounty, by helping others to properly backup all

With advances in technology, the number of hackers is also increasing day by day. While talking about of their lost data, learning the possible vulnerabilities within a system to make the administrators aware of the possible threats, among others.

By "hacker," it does not mean that they are the ones who can break into any form of restricted area within the world of cyber security; they are also IT experts who manage the security of a company or an organization. Most of the hackers are required to be anonymous at the time of hacking and they always try hard to make it difficult to detect them. There are various types of tools which are used by the hackers for hiding their identities such as VPN or Virtual Private Network, RDP or Remote Desktop Protocol and ProxyServers.

To perform a penetration test absolutely anonymously and to decrease the overall chances of detection, hackers are required to use some kind of intermediary machinery whose very own IP address will be left back on the system of the target. The hackers fulfill this motive by the use of proxy. A proxy server or proxy is a form of dedicated system of software or computer which also runs on a computer system and acts as the intermediary between a client's server and the end device like a computer system. By connecting with the Internet via the proxies, the IP address of the client system will not be displayed but the IP address of the proxy server will be shown in place of it. It helps in providing the clients with an increased amount of privacy when they connect directly with the internet.

The features of ProxyChains

The primary features of ProxyChains are:

- It supports SOCKS4, SOCKS5 along with HTTP CONNECT based proxy servers.
- The ProxyChains can be mixed up with any other type of proxy in the list.
- ProxyChains does support various methods of chaining such as: random in which any random proxy within the list which is stored within a file of configuration or chaining proxies in the similar list of order, the various form of proxies are kept separated from each other by the use of new line in the file. It also comes with a dynamic option in which the ProxyChains pass through only those proxies which are live in nature. It excludes any form of unreachable or dead proxy. This form of proxy is also known as the smart option.
- You can use the ProxyChains with servers such as sendmail, squid and many others.

- The ProxyChains also come with the ability of resolving DNS via the proxies.
- It can handle any form of TCP client application which is telnet, nmap and others.

Syntax of ProxyChains

In place of just running a simple penetration test or by creating various target requests directly by using your IP address, you can use ProxyChains for covering up and handling all these jobs. You will just need to add a command 'proxychains' for every job. This will enable the service of ProxyChains.

For instance, you want to scan some of the available hosts along with its ports in the network by the use of Nmap with ProxyChains, the command will look like:

proxychains nmap 192.168.0.0/25

The breakup of this command syntax will be:

proxychains: This will tell the machine to run the service of ProxyChains

nmap: Tells the ProxyChains about which jobs to be performed

192.168.0.0/25 or some other argument: It is the argument which is needed for any form of tool or job and in this case, it is your scan range which is needed for Nmap to run the scan.

How can ProxyChains be used?

Before you start to use ProxyChains, you will need to set up the configuration file for ProxyChains. You will also be requiring a list of the proxy servers. The configuration file of ProxyChains is located on /etc/proxychains.conf. Open up the file proxychains.conf in any text editor of your choice and then set up the overall configuration. By default settings, the proxychains will be directly sending the overall traffic first via your host at 127.0.0.1 on the port 9050 which is the default configuration for Tor. In case you are also using Tor, you can leave this whole thing as it is. If you are not using Tor, you will be required to comment this line out.

You will now need to add some more proxies. There are various free proxy servers that can be found on the Internet. Comment the proxy which is set by default for Tor. If you are not using it, then add the proxy on the config file of Proxychains and then save it.

Random_Chain VS Dynamic_Chain

A Random Chain will allow you to choose the IP addresses in a random way from the list. Every time you use ProxyChains, the chain of the proxy will be looking different to the target and thus making it more difficult to track down the traffic from the source.

In Dynamic Chain, you can run your traffic via every proxy on the list and in case any of the proxies is not responding or is down, the dead proxies are completely skipped out and it will automatically go for the next proxy in line without giving an error message. Each of the connections is done through the chained proxies. Each and every proxy on the list is chained in an order as they appear in that list.

Chapter 9: Virtual Private Networks

Virtual Private Network or VPN is one of the latest techniques of setting up a super secure form of connection along with another form of network directly over the internet. VPNs are being widely used today for the sole purpose of accessing various websites which are restricted in various regions, for protecting all the activities of browsing from the prying eyes of public Wi-Fi and many others. Today, VPNs are widely popular but in most cases, it is not
being used for the purpose for which it was developed. It was designed for connecting with the business network in a much more safe and secure way over the Web.

It also came on the market with the objective of allowing the users to access their business networks from their home only. This technique functions by forwarding all forms of traffic within a network by providing several benefits like accessing of local network resources remotely, bypassing any form of censorship on the web in some places, etc. Many of the operating systems which can be found today in the market also come with VPN pre-installed.

Benefits of using VPN

The concept on which VPN works is very easy and simple. It works by connecting a user directly with some other computer system or server over the internet. It then lets the user surf the contents available on the internet by bypassing and using the internet connection of that same server or computer. So, what makes VPN much more interesting is that if you have connected

with a computer from some other province or country, it will show that you are also from that same country. So, you will be now able to access anything by using VPN along with those things which you couldn't have done normally.
You can use a VPN for a wide collection of purposes:

- You can use VPN for the purpose of bypassing any restriction on any website which is based on province or geography. You can also use VPN streaming of audio and video.
- You can watch any form of online streaming such as Netflix, Hulu etc.
- You can protect yourself from the radars at the time of accessing torrents.
- You can protect yourself from connecting to any type of harmful Wi-Fi hotspot .
- You can gain a greater amount of privacy while online by simply hiding the actual location of your system.

Majority of the users of VPN use this technique for bypassing the restrictions on their geography to access the contents which are restricted by using a network of some other province. It is also used for accessing and downloading content via torrent. However, VPNs can be really helpful at the time of accessing any form of public Wi-Fi such as the ones available in railway stations or coffee shops.

How can you get a VPN?

The VPN that you need will depend completely on your usage and requirements. You can start by either creating a VPN server for yourself or out of your house. In case you want to create a VPN from work you can do that as well. In the real world, people look out for VPN for accessing the restricted contents which are banned in various countries and areas such as torrent. If you want a VPN for just surfing the restricted form of contents, you can download one from the internet according to your requirement.

How does a VPN work?
When you start by connecting any of your devices such as tablet, smartphone, laptop or desktop with the VPN, your device system will begin to behave as it is also from the same local form of network as the server of the VPN. The set of network traffic will be passed across a secure form of connection directly to the VPN. As your system will behave as if it is also from the similar network as the server, it will allow you to access all the resources of that same local
network in a highly secure way when you are accessing it from some other part of the world. You can also surf the internet as if you were present at the exact location of the VPN which comes with some additional form of privileges if you are using any public Wi-Fi or if you want to access any type of website which is geo-restricted.

While you start browsing the internet by being connected with the Virtual Private Network, your device will contact the network of the VPN while absolutely secured and encrypted in nature. VPNs help by forwarding the requests of the users and then bring back the response of the website across the secure connection. For instance, in case you are using a VPN from the UK for accessing Netflix contents, Netflix will see that your connection is coming from any state of the UK only.

You can also access any business network while you are on the go. While you connect with any business network while travelling, the local network resources are not at all required to be exposed to the Web and it also helps by improving the security of your business network.

Chapter 10: Introduction to Wireless Networking

While talking about networking, one of the most trending topics is wireless networking. It has allowed people to reach new heights of reliability, along with benefits which allow them to use the internet with their devices without any form of cable or wire in between. All of these have been possible only because of wireless networking. In wireless networking, all the devices connect with a network switch or router which helps in establishing connection between the devices and the Web via radio waves. All the information and connection are established through the air.

Thus, it can be regarded as a mobile form of network where you are no longer required to be seated in one single place for surfing the internet. Wireless networking comes with some very interesting features which will be discussed further in this chapter. So, let's start with wireless networking and its various features.

Hacking and Penetration Testing with Kali Linux

Each and every organization and company comes with certain weak points which might turn out to be malicious. Such weak points can also lead to some serious form of attack which can be later used for manipulation of organizational data.

The only thing that you are left with which can ultimately help you in preventing all forms of hackers from getting into your systems is regular checking of infrastructure security. You will also need to ensure that no form of vulnerability is present within the infrastructure. For serving all of these functions, penetration testing is something which can ultimately help you. It helps in detecting the vulnerabilities within a system and forwards the same information to the organization administrators for filling up the gaps. Penetration testing is always performed within a highly secure and real environment which helps in finding out the real form of vulnerabilities and then helps to secure the system.

Details about penetration testing
It is a process which is used for testing of the systems for finding out whether any third party can penetrate the system or not. Ethical hacking is often mixed up with penetration testing as both of them somewhat serve the similar purpose and also functions more or less in the same way. In penetration testing, the pen tester scans the systems for any form of system vulnerability, flaws, risks and malicious content. You can perform penetration testing either in an online form of environment or server or
even in a computer system. Penetration testing comes with the ultimate form of agendas: strengthening the system's security and defending the structure of an organization from potential attacks and threats.

Penetration testing is absolutely legal and is done along with the other official workings. When used in the proper and way, penetration testing has the ability of performing wonders. You can also consider penetration testing as a potential part of ethical hacking. You will need to perform the penetration tests at a regular intervals as it can improve the system capabilities. It also helps in improving cyber security. In order to find all the weak points within a program, system or application, various forms of malicious content are created by the pen testers. For an effective form of testing, the harmful form of content is spread across the overall network for the testing of vulnerability.

The technique used by penetration testing might not handle all the security concerns, but it can help to minimize the chances of attacks on the system. Penetration testing ensures that an organization or company is absolutely safe from all forms of threats and vulnerabilities and it helps in providing security from the cyber attacks. It also makes sure that the system of defense of an organization is working properly and is also enough for the company or organization to prevent the attacks and threats. It also indicates the security measures which are required to be changed by the organization to defend the system from attacks and vulnerabilities. All the reports regarding penetration testing are handed over to the system administrators.

Metasploit

Metasploit is nothing but a framework meant for penetration testing which actually makes the concept of hacking much easier. It is regarded as an important tool for the majority of the attackers along with the security defenders. All you need to do is to just point Metasploit at the target, pick any exploit of your choice, choose the payload which you want to drop and just hit Enter. However, it is not that casual in nature and so you will need to start from the beginning. Back in the golden days, the concept of penetration testing came with lots of repetitive forms of labor which is now being automated by the use of Metasploit.

What are the things that you need? Gathering of information or gaining of access or maintaining the levels of persistence or evading all forms of detection? Metasploit can be regarded as the Swiss knife for hackers; if you want to opt for information security as your future career then you are required to know this framework in detail. The core of the Metasploit framework is free in nature and also comes pre-installed with the software Kali Linux.

How to use Metasploit?
Metasploit can seamlessly integrate itself with SNMP scanning, Nmap and enumeration of Windows patch along with others. It also comes with a bridge to the Tenable's scanner of vulnerability along with Nessus. Most of the reconnaissance tools which you can think of can integrate along with Metasploit and thus it makes it possible to find the

strongest possible point in the shield of security. After you have identified the weakness in a system, you can start hunting across the huge and extensible database for a point of exploit which will help in cracking the strongest armor and will let you in the system. Just like the combination of cheese and wine, you can also pair an exploit with the payload for suiting any task at hand.

Most of the hackers are looking out for a shell. It is a proper payload at the time of attacking a system based on Windows which acts as the Meterpreter and also as an in-memory form of interactive shell. Linux comes with its own set of shellcodes which depends on the exploit being used. Once within a target machine, the quiver of Metasploit comes with a complete suite of post-exploitation tools which also includes escalation of privileges, pass the hash, screen capture, packet sniffing, pivoting and keylogger tools. If you want you can also easily set up a proper form of backdoor if the target machine gets rebooted somehow.

Metasploit is loaded up with more and more features each year along with a fuzzer for identifying the potential flaws of security in the binaries as well as a too long list of the modules which are of auxiliary nature. What we have discussed till now is only a high-level vision of what can be done with Metasploit. The overall framework is modular in nature and can be extended easily and it also enjoys an active form of community. If it is not doing what you want, you can easily tweak it to meeting your needs.

How can you learn Metasploit?
You can find various cheap as well as free resources for the purpose of learning Metasploit. The best way of starting with Metasploit is by downloading Kali Linux followed by the installation along with a virtual machine for practicing on the target.

The organization which maintains Kali Linux and also runs the OSCP certification, Offensive Security, offers a free course that includes training of Metasploit and is known as Metasploit Unleashed.

Where can you download Metasploit?

Metasploit can be found along with the hacking software Kali Linux. But, if you want you can also download it separately from the official website of Metasploit. Metasploit can be used on the systems which are based on Windows and *nix. You can find out the source code of Metasploit Framework on GitHub. Metasploit is also available in various forms on the internet.

Datastore

The datastore can be regarded as a core element of the Metasploit Framework. It is nothing but a table of several named values which allows the users to easily configure the component behavior within Metasploit. The datastore allows the interfaces to configure any of the settings, exploits for defining the parameters and also payloads for the purpose of patching the opcodes. It also allows Metasploit Framework to pass internally between the options of modules. You can find two types of datastores, the Global datastore which can be defined by using 'setg' and the Module datastore which can be defined at the modular level of datastore by using 'set'.

SQL Injection and Wi-Fi Hacking

When it comes to cyber attacks, one of the most widely used forms is the SQL Injection attack. In this, an attacker executes threat or invalid form of SQL statements which are used for database server control for an application of the web. It is also used for modifying, deleting or adding up records within the database without even the user knowing anything about it. This ultimately compromises the integrity of the data. The most important step which can be taken for avoiding or preventing SQL injection is by input validation.

SQL Injection and its types

There are various types of SQL injection which you can find today. Let's have a look at them.

- **Classic or In-band SQL injection:** 1. Error based: Attackers employ the generated error by the database to attack the database server.
  2. Union based: In this UNION SQL operator is employed for combining a response for returning to the HTTP response.
- **Inferential or Blind SQL injection:** 1. Based on Boolean: It is based on return of true or false.
  2. Time based: It sends out SQL injection which forces the database just before responding.
- **Out of band SQL injection:** This takes place when an attacker is unable to use the similar form of channel for attacking and gathering the results.

Tools used for SQL injection

There are various tools which are used for carrying out SQL injection.

- SQLMap: This tool is used for an automatic form of SQL injection and it helps in taking over the database.
- jSQL Injection: It is a Java based tool which is used for SQL injection.
- Blind-SQL-BitShifting: It is used for blind SQL injection by the use of BitShifting.
- BBQSQL: It is a blind form of SQL injection exploitation tool.
- explo: It is a format of machine and human readable web vulnerability testing.
- Whitewidow: It is a scanning tool which is used for checking out the vulnerabilities of the SQL database.
- Leviathan: It acts as an audio toolkit.
- Blisqy: It is used for the purpose of exploiting time-based SQL injection within the headers of HTTP.

Detection tools for SQL injection

A tool named Spider testing tool is widely used for the purpose of identifying the holes of SQL injection manually by the use of POST or GET requests. If you can resolve the vulnerabilities within the code then you can easily prevent the SQL injections. You can also use a web vulnerability scanner for identifying all the defects within the code and for fixing the same to prevent SQL injection. The firewalls present in the web application or within the application layer can also be used extensively for preventing any form of intrusion.

Hacking of Wi-Fi

Wi-Fi, or wireless networking, is the most preferred medium which is used for the purpose of network connectivity in today's world. However, because of its popularity, the wireless networks are also subjected to various attacks, along with several issues of security. If the attacker gains complete access to the network connection then the attacker can sniff off the data packets from any nearby location. The attackers employ sniffing tools for finding out the SSIDs and then hacks the Wi-Fi or wireless networks. After successful hacking, the attackers can monitor all the devices which are connected with the same SSID of the network. If you use authentication of WEP then it might be subject to dictionary attack. The attackers employ the RC4 encryption algorithm for the purpose of creating stream ciphers which are easily cracked. In case you are using authentication of WPA, then it might be subject to DOS along with dictionary attacks.

Tools for hacking of Wi-Fi

For the purpose of cracking WEP, the attackers use various tools such as WEPcrack, Aircrack, Kismet, WEPDecrypt and many others. For cracking WPA, tools such as Cain, Abel and CowPatty are used by the hackers. There are also other tools which are used in general for hacking of wireless network systems like wireshark, Airsnort, Wifiphisher, Netstumbler and many others. Even the attackers are now able to hack the mobile phone platform via the wireless network system. Android can be regarded as the most found mobile phone based platform but it is also very much susceptible to some specific types of vulnerabilities which ultimately makes it easier for the attackers to exploit the device security and then steal data from it. The most dangerous threats for the mobile devices are third party applications, email Trojans, wireless hacking and SMS.

How are Wi-Fi attacks carried out?

Most of the wireless network attacks are carried out by setting up rogue Access Points.

- **Evil Twin attack:** In this, the hacker sets up a false access point with the same name as that of the corporate AP which is close to the premises of the company. When any employee of the company connects to that access point, that employee unknowingly gives out all the details of authentication of the actual access point. Thus, the hacker can easily compromise the overall connection.
- **Signal jamming:** The hackers can easily disrupt the network connection which can be done by jamming the network signals. This is done by various tools which are used for creating noise.
- **Misconfiguration attack:** When the router of a network is set up by using a default form of configuration, weak form of encryption, weak credentials and algorithms, an attacker can easily crack the network.
- **Hotspot attack:** The attackers set up false hotspots or access points with the same name of the SSID similar to any public Wi-Fi access point. When any user connects with that access point unknowingly, the hackers can easily get access to the actual network.

How to Carry Out an Effective Attack

The term 'hacking' doesn't mean that it has to be negative all the time. You will have a proper idea about the overall process of hacking only when you will have a clear perception about the process behind it. Not only will you be able to learn about the process of hacking, but you will also be able to make your system much more protected from external attacks. Most of the time, when an attacker tries to gain access to a server of an organization or a company, it is generally done by using 5 proper steps. Let's have a look at those steps.

- **Reconnaissance:** This can be regarded as the very first step in the hacking process. During this phase, the attacker uses all the available means for the purpose of collecting all forms of relevant information about the primary target system. The relevant set of information might include the proper identification of the target, DNS records of the server, range of the IP address which is in target, the network and various other aspects. In simple terms, the attacker tries to collect all sorts of information along with the contacts of a website or server. This can be done by the attacker by the use of several forms of search engines like maltego or by researching about the system which is the target or by using the various tools like HTTPTrack to download a complete website for enumeration at a later stage.
By performing all these steps, the attacker will be able to determine the names of all the staffs within an organization very easily, find out the designated posts along with the email addresses of the employees.
- **Scanning:** After collecting all the relevant information about the target, the attacker will now start with the process of scanning. During this phase, the attacker employs various forms of tools like dialers, port scanners, vulnerability scanners, sweepers and network mappers for the purpose of scanning the target website or server data. During this step, the attackers try to seek out all the information which can actually help in the execution of a successful attack such as the IP address of the system, the user accounts and the computer names within that server. Right after the hackers are done with scanning of basic information, they start to test the target network to find out the possible avenues of attack. They might also employ several methods for network mapping just like Kali Linux.

The hackers also search for any automatic email system by which they can mail the staff of the target company about some false form of query like mailing the company HR about a job query.
- **Access gaining:** This is the most important of all the steps. In this phase, the attacker designs the blueprint of the target network along with the help of all relevant information which is collected in the first and second steps. As the hackers are done with enumeration of data followed by scanning of the system, they will now move to the step of gaining access to the system which will be based on the collected information.

- For instance, the attacker might decide to use a phishing attack. The attackers will always try to play safe and might employ a very simple attack for gaining overall access to the system. The attacker might also penetrate into the system from the IT department shell. The hackers use phishing email by employing the actual email address of the company. By using this phishing email ID, the attacker will send out emails to the techs that will also contain some form of specialized program
along with a phishing website for gathering information about the login passwords and IDs. For this, the attackers can use various methods such as phone app, website mail or something else and then asking the employees to login with their credentials into a new website.
As the hackers use this method, they already have a special type of program running in the background which is also called as Social Engineering Toolkit which is used for sending out emails with the address of the server to the users.
- **Maintaining access to the server:** After the attackers have gained access to the target server, they will try every

possible means for keeping their access to the server safe for future attacks and for the purpose of exploitation. As the attacker now has overall access to the server, he might also use the server as his very own base for launching several other forms of attacks. When an attacker gains access to an overall system and also owns the system, such a system is called as zombie system. The hacker might also try to hide himself within the server by creating a new administrator account with which he can easily mingle with the system without anyone knowing about it. For keeping safe access to the system, the hacker traces out all those accounts which are not being used for a long time and then elevates the privileges of all those accounts to himself.

As the hacker makes sure that no one has sensed his presence within the system, he starts to make copies of all the data on that server along with the contacts, messages, confidential files and many more for future use.

- **Clearance of tracks:** Right before starting with the attack, the hackers chalk out their entire track regarding the identity so that it is not possible for anyone to track them. The attackers begin by altering the system MAC address and then run their entire system via a VPN so that no one can trace their actual identity.

Conclusion

As you have completed learning the teachings of this entire eBook, you now have a very clear perception of the concepts of hacking along with the processes linked with it. You must have also gained a lot of knowledge about the properties, functioning and usage of Kali Linux. After completing this book, you will also be able to frame up all the necessary tools along with the components needed for setting up a secure and safe server of network meant either for your business or for your personal use. Always keep one thing in mind; you are the one who is responsible for everything that happens with your network or server.

With the help of Kali Linux, plus its relevant tools, you will be able to have a complete grip over the interface of your network security. This whole eBook is not only about the aspects of Kali Linux, it also discusses the basics of networking along with its security. With the help of Kali Linux, you will be able to perform periodic penetration testing which will ultimately determine the security of your system.

So, if you are thinking about improving the security of your network server, then start right away with the help of this eBook along with Kali Linux. Remember, you are the one who can actually make or break the security wall of your network.

If you find this book helpful for your business in any way, kindly leave a review on Amazon.